A Miracle for Angelo

FINDING HOPE IN THE STORY OF THE MANGER

JOANNA ZEINER

LUCIDBOOKS

A Miracle for Angelo
Finding Hope in the Story of the Manger

Copyright © 2019 by Joanna Zeiner
Headshot by Eddie Kirkham Photography, Uvalde, TX

Published by Lucid Books in Houston, TX
www.LucidBooksPublishing.com

ISBN-10: 1-63296-369-8
ISBN-13: 978-1-63296-369-7
eISBN-10: 1-63296-359-0
eISBN-13: 978-1-63296-359-8

Special Sales: Most Lucid Books titles are available in special quantity discounts. Custom imprinting or excerpting can also be done to fit special needs. Contact Lucid Books at Info@LucidBooksPublishing.com.

"A Miracle for Angelo describes a crisis of faith in the context of family relations, a life crisis, human blame of the Divine, and resolution in a Christmas miracle. Joanna intriguingly describes the life of a small fictional town, Greccio, Italy, showing how the simple life of simple people in a small community transcends the centuries and parallels the human search for significance today. Human and divine experience is presented honestly in this short story, which applies anytime, anywhere for all people who may be desperate to find answers to the age-old question: "Why, God, did you do that?" In your crisis of faith, this story speaks about the helplessness of the human and the power of God to be with those who are willing to listen well to their hearts and to the Christ of the manger. Read it to yourself; read it to your children and to your children's children."

—**Ilya A. Okhotnikov**, PhD, DMin, CFLE-P,
Assistant Professor of Family Science,
Program Coordinator, McNeese State University
Department of Social Sciences

"Joanna's simple story of Angelo, Marianna, and Maria draws us quickly into deep joy and then into anguished loss as we watch Angelo's heart harden into stone with unresolved grief and anger. Angelo's story is Joanna's story; it is our story, too. Only God can break open and release such a heart—God who listens to the cries of our hearts, God who became one of us through the miracle of incarnation. Prepare to have your heart pierced by God who meets you right where you live."

—**The Reverend Dr. Sandra B. Kerner**

"I loved reading *A Miracle for Angelo*. In the true sense of the word, it is sweet and rich, a gem of a story with a timeless appeal to experience the love that came down at Christmas—and stayed with us."

—**The Reverend Dr. Russ Parker**,
Author of *Healing Wounded History*

"Short, riveting, powerful—packed with truth and revelation of the kindness of the Father. This little book is a perfect Christmas gift for all the "Angelos" in your life because it points us to The Perfect Christmas Gift—the One who came in an unexpected manner and will come again likewise."

—**Suzanne Jones**,
Chief Operations Officer of
Cornerstone International

"Angelo's story will touch every reader in some personal way, for who has not, at some moment in time, believed that God could have done better for them? Reading this book will help identify the path to healing for those still struggling as a result of this belief. The author's personal account in the Preface is the first clue to this truth."

—**Denise Dolff, MA,**
Retired Psychotherapist, Waterloo,
ON, Canada

"This delightful book will open your heart to the depths and heights of God's love even in currently inexplicable moments. The joy of God living among us has changed everything forever."

—Bishop Sean Larkin

"Joanna Zeiner takes us straight into the home and into the hearts of this 13th century Italian family—who really are you and me. I saw my own dad in the character of Angelo. This story is poignant and powerful. I pray that the gentle Holy Spirit will take this profound offering and use it to heal our deepest places of bitterness. The reflection questions offer readers a safe place to quietly honor their own stories. I offer you this book with joy and great hope."

—Melanie Williams,
National Director of Aloe Christian Foundation,
South Africa

"Grief comes in all shapes and seasons. This short story by Joanna paints a tangible picture of grief, which is difficult to do in a measured number of words. The story is also, obviously, a story of redemption and hope, and through plot twists and turns, beautiful word pictures, and a poignant and unexpected ending, Joanna is able to bring it all round to the hopeful healing from the bitterness of grief and to soul redemption, which the reader prays that the main character, Angelo, will find. Well done!"

—Carol Lee,
Reaching Africa's Unreached (RAU)

"Many of us know the experience of shattered faith. I reached a point when losses and failures made a loving God inconceivable. I felt betrayed. In this simple, powerful story told through the lives of Angelo, Marianna, and Maria with beautiful, poetic imagery, Joanna Zeiner touched that place in me where I have been met by Love in the midst of despair. My tears confirmed the authenticity of this tale and its telling."

—Douglas W. Schoeninger, PhD,
Psychotherapist

"Joanna has used her writing skill to craft a beautiful story about the working of grace on a broken life. For all who have been wounded in this mortal life, and that includes most of us, this gentle story is one of healing and hope."

—Reverend Canon Michael Mitton,
Freelance writer, speaker, spiritual director

Contents

Preface

My daddy died when I was 15. I wasn't ready for it, but then, who is ready for a parent to die suddenly of a heart attack? Tears didn't come until the night before the funeral, and then they wouldn't stop. Eventually, a friend of the family came into my room, sat on the side of my bed, and said, "Joanna, what do you think your daddy would think to see you carrying on this way?" My tears dried up and remained well hidden for years, and I steadily pulled away, developed emotional outbursts, and became depressed. Through events and honest friends, I began to realize that my untended grief had morphed into a deep-set anger at Daddy for leaving me and at God for taking him away. That revelation broke my heart, yet it freed me. When I forgave Daddy for leaving me and got right with God again, the depression went away—not suddenly, but truly.

Later, at a Christmas dinner, I heard the story of the first live Christmas nativity. It was told from the point of view of one who understood God's love for the first time as found in the baby in the manger. That story personalized within me, and Angelo began coming to life.

Angelo was an honest person we all can relate to, albeit everyone in their own unique way. He faced a real personal crisis and had doubts. God was there for him, even though he couldn't see or hear Him because of the emotional detritus within. Angelo, a fictional character, is no man, and yet he is every man with struggles that obscure vision and endanger the soul. God met Angelo with an eternal truth that brought him—body and soul—to his knees. What better place for God to speak than in the lowliness of the manger.

A Miracle for Angelo is not a Christmas story although it is set within the first live nativity scene. It is a story of hope and inner peace. I trust this little story will speak a bit of peace to your heart.

Chapter 1

Long ago, Angelo, a sculptor of marble, lived in a hillside village deep in the Reiti Valley about 60 kilometers northeast of Rome. He was a simple man in much the same way that Greccio was a simple village whose inhabitants contented themselves with the simple pleasures of life. Rumors of medieval growth and change throughout Italy and farther in Europe whispered but did not intrude into the tranquility of Greccio's ancient stone walls. In the same simple way, Angelo was content with his love of stone, his family, and his uncomplicated faith in the goodness of God.

Each day, Angelo could be found in his small workshop where he had learned his stone craft from his father, who had learned it from his father before him. If one listened closely, one might hear the stonework in Greccio whisper stories of how Angelo's great-grandfathers worked by the sweat of their brows and the love of their craft.

But unlike his teachers, who cut blocks for houses or paving for cobbled streets, Angelo seemed to see within each untouched block of marble a creation that wanted to spring forth. For hours at a time, sometimes deep into the night when his oil lamp cast shadows on his workshop walls, he caressed the stone, lightly chipping here, his file smoothing there, until something of exceptional beauty emerged with an apparent life of its own. In testament to Angelo's craftsmanship, lords who were both secular and religious, military and academic knew the road that dipped into the Reiti Valley, wound up to the village of Greccio, and ended at Angelo's workshop.

The only thing Angelo loved more than his stone was Marianna, the younger sister of his best friend, Paulo. Angelo loved everything about Marianna—her sweet nature, peaceful smile, ability to laugh at the young boys' merciless teasing, and her understanding of his youthful, awkward attempts to demonstrate his affection for her. Eventually, Angelo married Marianna, and theirs was a happy, peaceful home for one year and two, then three years, slowly moving on to five and six.

Only one thing lacked in their life together, one thing that overshadowed their joy. There were no children. Angelo felt great sorrow. But most of all, he grieved for Marianna. Each year with no child, the easy laughter and mischievous spark that had accompanied her into womanhood faded into a heartbreak Angelo found more and more unable to bear. He tried to tell her that it didn't matter that they had no children, that he loved her enough for a dozen children. But her heartache grew with the years, and Angelo knew it did matter very much.

Chapter 2

J ust when Angelo and Marianna had almost giv-
en up hope that their prayers for a child would
ever be heard, God gave them a miracle—a baby
daughter born just three weeks before Christmas. It
was said by those who seemed to know such things
that at the baby's birth, angels hovered near just to
gaze on the child's perfection and wonder at the cre-
ative hand of her Maker. The whole village of Greccio gathered around the family and rejoiced with
Marianna, Angelo, and the little baby they named
Maria, in honor of the mother of Christ.

As Maria grew, Marianna's heartbreak healed;
her smile returned as did her quiet, ever-patient
love of life. Maria's dancing brown eyes, so like
Marianna's, and her rose-flushed cheeks began to
change Angelo as well. He took time from his work

to play with Maria, and he laughed out loud for
no reason at all. Angelo's love for Maria filled his
strong, barrel chest so much that at times it seemed
he could hardly breathe.

When the child no longer required Marianna's
constant care, Angelo took her for walks through
the village and further out into the countryside.
"Come, my angel. I have to run an errand to the far
side of the village. Do you want to come with me?"

"How far are we going, Papá?" Every time
Maria joined her father for a walk, she asked that
same question. It had now become a game, one
they both enjoyed playing with each other. Each
time, Angelo answered her the same: "Until we
find a miracle as wonderful as you, my angel." The
townspeople, so used to seeing Angelo purposefully
maneuvering the streets on one errand or another,
smiled as he ambled alongside Maria, his large
calloused hand gently cradling her childish grip,
his long-reaching strides shortened to fit her own
tripping steps. When she tired, Angelo swung her
onto his powerful shoulders as effortlessly as the
moon rising at twilight or the sun at dawn. Father
and daughter searched often for that miracle as
wonderful as she, but finding none, they contented

themselves with gathering wildflowers in spring to set on the wooden table in Marianna's cozy kitchen. Sometimes, they simply sat under an olive tree and listened to the buzzing of bees in the warm autumn sunshine. Angelo and Maria were as inseparable as a rainbow and a promise.

Chapter 3

Everything changed when disaster struck Angelo's little family late in the year 1220. Along with the winter chill that filtered through the stone walls of their small home, a fever wrapped Maria in its fiery embrace. She hovered near death for days, fever burning her body and confusing her mind. "How far … going, Papá?" whimpered Maria in fever-induced delirium. "Mamá … found … no … miracle … flowers." Angelo and Marianna fought alone through their desperate fears for Maria. Neither seemed to have the strength of heart to support the other. Marianna repeatedly cleaned their already immaculate home, cooked meals that remained uneaten, and stared with red-rimmed eyes at the last dry sprigs of foliage that Maria had placed in an earthenware vase on the kitchen table.

Angelo could not work; he could not eat. He spent all his days either at Maria's bedside or in Greccio's small stone chapel praying. "God, You gave us a miracle when Maria was born. Please give us another miracle. Don't take her away from us. I'll do anything, but please don't take her away." Angelo offered prayers with such weeping that pools of tears gathered on the flagstone in front of the altar. He promised to make a new baptismal font for the chapel out of the purest white marble. He vowed to attend mass for the rest of his life. Give God something, and He'll give back to you, right?

Early one morning, Maria's fever finally broke, and she slipped into a deep but peaceful sleep. Marianna crumpled by Maria's bedside, her tears wetting Maria's limp, colorless hand. Angelo, beside himself with relief and not knowing exactly what to do, ran to the chapel and threw himself down before the stone altar with happy tears freely and unashamedly streaking his face. God had heard. Exhausted from lack of sleep and worry, Angelo eventually stumbled home and renewed his vigil by his daughter's bedside, content to watch her sleep.

Eventually, Maria stirred. Her eyes fluttered like tiny bird wings easing from their restrictive shell. "Yes, Maria." Angelo leaned closer to hear the whispers escaping through her tiny lips. Her words came slowly, two full heartbeats between each labored effort. "What is it you say?" Angelo asked. "I'm here, my angel."

"Papá, is that you? I hear … voice … Papá, where are you?" Her strength faltered, but she licked her lips and continued. "Please … light candle … I can't see … face. Papá? Mamá?"

Confusion melted into horror in the space of a single, unbelieving thought. Noon had passed, and the midday sun was arching its course to the west. There was light—plenty of light—but Maria could not see it. "Oh, God, no," Marianna whispered. "No!" The departing fever had taken with it Maria's sight.

Chapter 4

In the months that followed, Maria gradually regained her strength, and her skin softened once again into a porcelain rose. Spring's wildflowers replaced the chill of winter snow again and yet again. Life moved on in Angelo's home. Marianna found some sense of purpose as she cared for her daughter and kept her home. She took her questions to the stone altar in the chapel and seemed to leave them there. As Maria learned to deal with her blindness, she grew lovelier with a delicate sense of grace and peace. Peace, however, did not come to Angelo.

He devoted himself to Maria's every desire. They still walked hand-in-hand through the village streets, and in spring, they gathered wildflowers for Marianna's kitchen. But when Maria asked, "How far are we going, Papá?" Angelo refused to answer. Something had changed, something he didn't even understand himself.

To say he was terribly disappointed by Maria's blindness did not convey the intense anger that seized his heart. He feared for her—feared she would never know the fullness of life and beauty that had begun to flourish in her before the fever burned it away. Driven almost to the point of madness, he vented his fear as rage. Stone fragments littered the workshop like the shards of his dreams for Maria. His hands grew heavy and careless, the chisel more often breaking than coaxing the stone. To Angelo, the obvious one to blame for Maria's blindness was God. After all, God should have done more for his little girl, or so Angelo chose to believe.

Marianna cracked open the outside door to Angelo's workshop and asked for the thousandth time, "Won't you come to mass today with Maria and me?" Angelo slowly drew himself up from his work and exhaled a deep breath. He stared coldly at Marianna, and then his glare strayed to Maria who stood outside near her mother, her hand gently clutching Marianna's robe. Maria looked heavenward; her sightless eyes appeared to trace the path of a white puffball cloud chasing across the sky. Angelo's quiet voice belied his barely restrained rage.

"We prayed for a miracle for Maria. Some miracle! Is this a good God who takes a perfect child and plunges her into darkness for the rest of her life? Do not speak to me of God." The chasm that had grown between them deepened as Marianna turned to leave with Maria for the little stone chapel, and Angelo returned to his cold, uncut stone.

Their turning away grieved Marianna for it created a distance between them for the first time in their lives. Young Angelo had never openly spoken of his affection for her—it was hard for him to voice his feelings—yet she knew. She had secretly loved him, even when he, as a boy, raced in and out of the house with Paulo. As the youngest child in a home of three brothers, Marianna could have easily ended up spoiled. But life in Greccio was too hard for spoiling. Marianna grew adept at listening, watching, and waiting, thus learning well how to stem the budding contention always present in a home with older siblings.

Marianna understood Angelo better than he

knew himself. A sculptor's road is as hard as the stone he depends on for a living. Even after they married, life remained difficult for the young couple. But Marianna and Angelo had always depended on each another, even in the hardest of times. After Maria came, the three of them were as close as a three-strand cord—until now. Angelo had distanced himself from Marianna, although she was sure he really didn't know he had done so.

Chapter 5

In December 1223, Maria turned 12. By now, she carried her darkness like a soft, woolen scarf around her slim shoulders—lightly with hardly a sense of limitation or loss. Her heightened sense of hearing and touch grew so fine that people again wondered if there were angels hovering around and quietly whispering in her ear. Angelo heard these rumors, and it angered him. Maria needed no angels; she had him. And to prove how much he loved and cherished her, he determined that for Christmas he would make Maria a very special gift, a perfect gift that only he could create. He shut himself in his workshop, not letting anyone come in, sleeping very little, eating even less. Slowly, his gift took shape until, just three days before Christmas, he laid his tools down for the last time and called Marianna into his workshop.

"Angelo, it's exquisite! I've never seen anything so beautiful!" Marianna whispered as if she were afraid that a spoken word might awaken the sleeping baby. "I feel as if it will move or cry out. Maria will love it." Marianna cradled in her arms a perfect doll sculpted from the purest, white marble, smaller than life-size so it would not be too heavy for Maria to hold but so real that it seemed to breathe. Yes, Maria would surely love it! Angelo took the doll, wrapped it in a soft, woolen blanket, and placed it on the shelf above his workbench until Christmas Day when he—and he alone—would place it in Maria's arms.

The next day, an unusual little procession wound through the streets of Greccio, stopping finally at the entrance of the village's small, stone chapel. A holy man, barefoot and dressed in black, homespun wool, led an ox, a donkey laden with hay, and a growing menagerie of children, curious adults, and tail-wagging village mongrels.

"Is it him?"

"Yes, I believe so."

"No, it can't be him here in our village."

"But who else could it be?"

Everyone had heard of Francisco di Bernadone,

the son of a wealthy Assisi cloth merchant who had turned away from a privileged life to walk the roads of poverty with those less fortunate than he. Some knew him as God's Troubadour, others simply as Francis of Assisi.

"What is he doing here in our village?" The growing mob held their curiosity to a polite murmur until one brave soul stepped forward.

"Welcome to our humble village, Brother. To what do we owe such a privilege?"

"Privilege? No, you owe nothing for our presence among you. Rather, we ask that you receive our own humble company to celebrate together our Lord's most holy Christmas mass."

Polite murmurs swelled into a chorus of anticipation that echoed into the farthest corners and households of Greccio. Like bees humming around the hive, voices buzzed with the amazing news.

"You must come to Christmas Eve mass. It is going to be different."

"I don't know what will happen, but the holy man said it will be special. Yes, it is Brother Francis himself who says it will be different from any Christmas mass we have ever known! What can it all mean?"

Francis walked the streets of Greccio, inviting every man, woman, and child to join him for the Christmas Eve mass. In one fashion or another, they all said, "Yes, thank you, I'll be happy to come." Some adults watched from doorways; others whispered their curiosity while huddled in the street. Children frolicked and trailed him wherever he went, and even the sparrows swirled around his head like a halo as if they, too, wanted to be near him. But when the monk's shadow fell across the entrance of Angelo's workshop, the door closed soundly. Angelo wanted nothing to do with this messenger of a God who had so cruelly betrayed him and blinded his Maria.

Christmas Eve arrived in a peak of excitement among the people of Greccio, and soon it became evident that the chapel would not hold the crowds expected to come to the midnight mass. So Francis determined to hold his service in the rock grotto near the town square so everyone attending could see. Late in the day, Marianna approached her husband. "Angelo, the holy man has asked if anyone has a baby that can be used in the service tonight. There are no infants among the villagers, so I was wondering, would you consent to let him use the doll you made for Maria?"

"Absolutely not! If he is such a holy man, let him pray and ask God for a baby to fall from the sky. That would be a miracle, no? My doll is not for God; it is for Maria's hands alone. No one else is even to touch it." Marianna's heart broke to hear Angelo's angry ravings, but she knew for now to say no more.

Later that evening, as Marianna and Maria prepared to leave, Marianna attempted once again to approach Angelo. "Will you not join us tonight for the Christmas Eve Mass? It is to be a very special celebration of the Christ child's birth."

"Yes, please, Papá. Do join us," begged Maria. The deep pools of her eyes reflected a secret that he didn't understand. There had never been any secrets between them. Unsettled and confused, he growled incoherently and stormed into the winter-clear night without a coat.

For an hour, he wandered the abandoned streets and alleyways of Greccio. It seemed that everyone had gone to the mass—everyone except him, that is. The cobbled streets grabbed at his stumbling feet; high stone walls of the houses and empty shops crowded coldly around his heart as if the very stone itself tried to speak into his troubled mind. "Angelo, mark what you do." What was that? Angelo turned around to see who had spoken. But no one appeared. "Angelo, mark what you do." Again, the whisper, but this time he knew it came from his own heart, for hadn't his father always said, "Angelo, mark what you do" when the young apprentice was about to make a wrong cut in the stone? His nerves chased the midnight chill through his body as he tried to block the words that kept trolling through his mind. Only one place offered Angelo any solace, so he quickly made his way back to his workshop and lit a small oil lamp. He reached up to the shelf above his workbench where lay Maria's doll.

"What is this?" Angelo's groping hands searched the shelf from back to front, from side to side. Refusing to believe, he lit another lamp. "The doll is gone. Where? Who?" Clarity burned through him like a summer wildfire. "She took it! Even after I said no, she betrayed me and took it." Angelo stormed out of his workshop and marked heavy steps toward the town square. As he approached the crowd, he heard the monk saying something, but Angelo was too far away and much too distracted to understand. The resisting mob oozed around Angelo as he elbowed his way forward.

"Get out of my way! Move over!" Like molten rock punching through the final barrier before erupting into the air, Angelo broke through the mob and prepared to launch himself at the monk who had dared defile his gift. Something stopped him cold. Francis stood beside a makeshift altar built into the grotto, and to his right lay an ox slowly chewing her cud with her sleeping calf, born out of season, curled into her soft, warm underbelly. A small, floppy-eared donkey stood nodding near sleep at Francis's feet. To the monk's left stood a crude wooden manger, and behind the manger lay a ewe and—did his eyes deceive him?— her newborn lamb snuggled in the soft, fresh-thrown hay. Transfixed, Angelo watched as Francis reached over and took from the manger—yes, there it was as he thought—the same woolen blanket he had wrapped around his beautiful marble doll. Angelo started to cry out, "Don't touch it! It's not yours!" but his tongue would not move. He could only watch as Francis gathered the doll in his arms, careful not to touch the glistening white marble, his tears wetting the swaddling blanket as he gazed into its perfect face. With trembling hands, Francis reached across to a small, robed figure sitting beside the manger and gently laid the doll in the arms of none other than Angelo's Maria.

Maria gasped as she felt the doll, her hands tenderly exploring the cool, perfect contours of its face, its tiny ears, and its slumbering form. She settled the doll against her own porcelain-like cheek and gently rocked back and forth, patting its back as if it were a real baby sleeping in its mother's arms.

In the silence of that clear, midnight sky, Francis chanted the gospel to the mesmerized crowd. He spoke of the Christmas story and the babe of Bethlehem—about how God chose to express His love for each man, woman, and child by giving His own Son to live among ordinary people to share their life, their poverty, their joys, their sorrows. The manger scene's simple witness pierced Angelo's heart, and for the first time in many years, tears welled in his grief-stricken eyes. And he understood. His anger at God had masked his own helplessness in not being able to protect

Maria from suffering and pain. Tears flowed as his heart broke, only this time, the words that filled his mind were not "God should have done more for my little girl." Now he heard his own heart-rending confession, "I couldn't do more for my little girl." As Maria had grown in grace and beauty, even in her blindness, guilt had eaten into his heart, and he had felt her slipping away. She flourished in a place he could not seem to go, and now again, Angelo feared he would lose her.

Angelo tore his eyes away from the manger scene only to find Francis gazing at him with eyes that shone with all the love and compassion God had for the poor sculptor—eyes that seemed to say, "I, too, have fought the battle of faith." As Francis stood beside the manger that had so recently held Angelo's doll, he held in his prayer-folded hands the simple, wooden crucifix that had stood on the altar. Angelo crumbled to his knees, chest heaving as years of anger and sorrow released from his heart. He saw for the first time that God really did know a father's anguish when seeing his child suffer. Peace began to wash through Angelo's tormented mind. Once again, he seemed to hear Maria's childish voice say, "How far are we going, Papá?" That night, during the first live Christmas nativity, Angelo began his own personal journey into the greatest miracle of all.

* * * * * * * *

Who among us will celebrate Christmas
right?
Those who finally lay down all their
power, honor, and prestige,
all their vanity, pride, and self-will
at the manger,
those who stand by the lowly and let God
alone be exalted,
those who see in the child in the manger
the glory of God
precisely in this lowliness. *

---

* Dietrich Bonhoeffer, ed. Manfred Weber, trans. Peter Heinegg, *The Mystery of Holy Night* (New York: The Crossroad Publishing Company, 1997), 17.

Discussion Questions

1. **Was there a key issue in Angelo's story that spoke personally to you? What was it? Identify and own it.** (This might be positive or negative; it might include something you have fought through or something that still bothers you.)

2. **Is there an appropriate course of action you feel you can take to address this key issue? Express it. Commit to following through.** (This is deeply personal to you.)

3. **How do you feel now that you have identified your key issue and committed to a course of action?** (Take time to let your mind and heart come together. Trouble comes when we remain cerebral and disconnected with our heart.)

4. **Sometimes, our concerns are too weighty to handle alone. Do not hesitate to locate a trusted listener or counselor to help you move forward.**

www.ingramcontent.com/pod-product-compliance
Lightning Source LLC
Chambersburg PA
CBHW061758040426
42447CB00011B/2368